A Little Book of

WISDOM

JARROLD
PUBLISHING

CONCERT DE FAMILLE

Jacob Jordaens 1593–1678

ALL WORDS are pegs to
hang ideas on.

HENRY WARD BEECHER

Never look back unless
you are planning to go that way.

ANON

Often the test of courage
is not to die but to live.

VITTORIO ALFIERI

The fool doth think he is wise, but the wise man
knows himself to be a fool.

WILLIAM SHAKESPEARE

IT MATTERS not how long you live, but how well.

PUBLILIUS SYRUS

Anyone can win –
unless there happens to be
a second entry.

GEORGE ADE

TWELFTH NIGHT, ACT II, SCENE IV
Walter Howell Deverell 1827–1854

If you ever find happiness by hunting for it,
you will find it, as the old woman did
her lost spectacles, safe on her own nose
all the time.

JOSH BILLINGS

Do not assume the other fellow has intelligence to
match yours. He may have more.

TERRY-THOMAS

To AVOID dandruff falling
on your shoulders, step nimbly to one side.

GEORGE BURNS

It is never too late to be
what you might have been.
GEORGE ELIOT

YOU'VE GOT to do your own growing,
no matter how tall your grandfather was.
ANON

Time is a great teacher,
but unfortunately it kills all its pupils.
HECTOR BERLIOZ

THE BOOK WORM
Karl Spitzweg
1808–1885

PHILIP IN CHURCH
Frederick Walker 1840–1875

WE SHOULD be careful to get out of an
experience only the wisdom that is in it –
and stop there, lest we be like the cat that sits
down on a hot stovelid. She will never sit down
on a hot stovelid again – and that is well; but also
she will never sit down on a cold one anymore.

MARK TWAIN

*S*cience may be learned by rote,
but Wisdom not.

LAURENCE STERNE

The longer we dwell on our misfortunes
the greater is their power to harm us.

VOLTAIRE

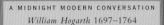

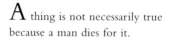

A thing is not necessarily true
because a man dies for it.

OSCAR WILDE

WISE MEN learn by other men's mistakes,
fools by their own.

ANON

READING THE NOVEL BY MANZONI,
THE PROMESSI SPOSI
Emilio de Amenti 1845–1885

EVERY PRODUCTION of genius must
be the production of enthusiasm.

BENJAMIN DISRAELI

The way I see it,
if you want the rainbow,
you gotta put up with the rain.

DOLLY PARTON

If you want your children to listen,
try talking softly – to someone else.

ANN LANDERS

ONLY TWO THINGS are infinite, the universe and human
stupidity, and I'm not sure about the former.

ALBERT EINSTEIN

*M*an is a history-making creature
who can neither repeat his past nor leave it behind.

W. H. AUDEN

*A*s I grow older I find that though I think
I'm saying the same things as I always did,
people listen to me more.

PETER USTINOV

A CHILD can ask questions
that a wise man cannot answer.

ANON

ARTHUR, DUKE OF WELLINGTON, WITH
GRANDCHILDREN IN LIBRARY AT STRATFIELD SAYE

Archibald Thorburn

VISITORS
Edgar Bundy 1862–1922

*N*obody can make you feel inferior
without your consent.

ELEANOR ROOSEVELT

T alk low, talk slow
and don't say too much.

JOHN WAYNE

THERE ARE many ways to die in bed,
but the best way is not alone.

GEORGE BURNS

My formula for living is quite simple.
I get up in the morning and I go to bed at night.
In between, I occupy myself as best I can.

CARY GRANT

In youth we learn; in age we understand.

MARIE EBNER-ESCHBACH

The tragedy of life doesn't lie in not
reaching your goal. The tragedy lies in
having no goal to reach.

BENJAMIN E. MAYS

THE MOTHER
Silvestro Lega 1826–1895

PHILOSOPHERS OF THE ANCIENT WORLD
– PLATO, PYTHAGORAS AND SOLON
Sucevita Monastery Rumania 1357

Nothing in life is to be feared,
it is only to be understood.

MARIE CURIE

WISE MEN talk because they have
something to say; fools talk because
they have to say something.

PLATO

Information is the most valuable commodity not
only to collect but to pass on.

VIOLET PATIENCE

THE THREE AGES OF MAN
Giorgione 1478–1510

Time is a physician that heals every grief.

DIPHILIUS

The sound of a kiss is not so loud as that of a cannon, but its echo lasts a great deal longer.

OLIVER WENDELL HOLMES

WE DO NOT inherit the earth from our ancestors; we borrow it from our children.

KENYAN PROVERB

THE GIANT SNOWBALL
Jean Mayne 1850–1905

Snowflakes are one of nature's
most fragile things, but just look what
they can do when they stick together.

VESTA M. KELLY

The less people know,
the more stubbornly they know it.

GEORGE ARTHUR

Death is just life's last great adventure.

VIOLET PATIENCE

Although the world is full of suffering,
it is also full of the overcoming of it.

HELEN KELLER

Old men must die, or the world
would grow mouldy, would only
breed the past again.

TENNYSON

Whoever is happy will make others happy too.

ANNE FRANK

THE HAPPY FRIAR
Giacimo de Chirico 1845–1884

GROUP OF TEN SEATED ANGELS
Ridolfo di Arpo Guariento d.1378

A short saying often
contains much wisdom.

SOPHOCLES

Luck is a matter of preparation
meeting opportunity.

OPRAH WINFREY

Life is a great surprise. I do not see why death
should not be an even greater one.

VLADIMIR NABOKOV

If a man shouts, his words no longer matter.

PETER USTINOV

 Man arrives as a novice at each age of his life.

NICOLAS CHAMFORT

TOO MANY people think they have an open mind when it's just vacant.

ANON

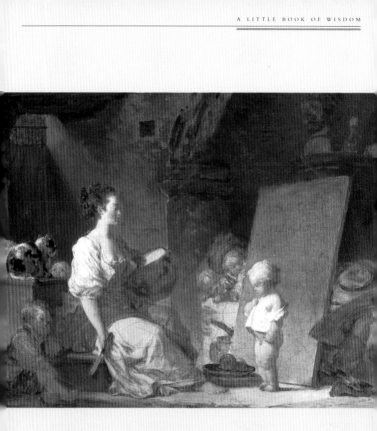

SAY PLEASE

Jean-Honoré Fragonard 1732–1806

THE FROWN

Thomas Webster 1800–1886

*G*enius is one per cent inspiration, ninety-nine per cent perspiration.

THOMAS ALVA EDISON

Six feet of earth make all men equal.

JAMES HOWELL

EXPERIENCE – a comb life gives you after you lose your hair.

JUDITH STERN

It is sad to grow old but nice to ripen.

BRIGITTE BARDOT

THERE IS A VERY easy way to return
from a casino with a small fortune —
go there with a large one.

JACK YELTON

Advice is like snow; the softer it falls,
the longer it dwells upon, and the deeper
it sinks into, the mind.

SAMUEL TAYLOR COLERIDGE

JANUARY OR AQUARIUS WITH COURTIERS
IN SNOWBALL FIGHT OUTSIDE STENICO CASTLE
Fresco from Cycle of Months c. 1400

SENECA, ROMAN STATESMAN AND PHILOSOPHER

55 BC

Those who cannot remember the past
are condemned to repeat it.

GEORGE SANTAYANA

A memorandum is written
not to inform the reader
but to protect the writer.

DEAN ACHESON

MANY PERSONS might have attained to wisdom had
they not assumed that they already possessed it.

SENECA

A lie can be half-way round the world
before the truth has got its boots on.

JAMES CALLAGHAN

*R*eal knowledge is to know
the extent of one's ignorance.

CONFUCIUS

*C*onsider the postage stamp, my son.
It secures success through its ability to stick
to one thing till it gets there.

JOSH BILLINGS

COMMON SENSE is the collection of
prejudices acquired by age eighteen.

ALBERT EINSTEIN

*A*n empty stomach
is not a good political adviser.

ALBERT EINSTEIN

ALBERT EINSTEIN, PLAYING THE PIANO

1933

Also in this series
Little Book of Humorous Quotations
Little Book of Naughty Quotations
Little Book of Wit

Also available
William Shakespeare Quotations
Winston Churchill Quotations

First published in Great Britain in 1997 by
Jarrold Publishing Ltd
Whitefriars, Norwich NR3 1TR

Developed and produced by
The Bridgewater Book Company

Researched and edited by David Notley
Picture research by Vanessa Fletcher
Printed and bound in Belgium 2/99

© Jarrold Publishing 1997. Reprinted 1999

ISBN 0-7117-0985-8

Acknowledgements

Jarrold Publishing Ltd would like to thank all those who kindly gave permission to
reproduce the words and visual material in this book; copyright holders have been
identified where possible and we apologise for any inadvertent omissions.

We would particularly like to thank the following for the use of pictures:
The Bridgeman Art Library, Corbis-Bettmann, e. t. archive,
Fine Art Photographic, Mary Evans Picture Library.

Front Cover: *Philip in Church*, Frederick Walker, 1840–1875
(e.t. archive)
Frontispiece: *Sakgamuni, Confucius and Lao Tzu*, Wang Shu-Ku painting,
18th century (e.t archive)
Back Cover: *Arthur, Duke of Wellington, with Grandchildren in Library at
Stratfield Saye*, Archibald Thorburn (e.t. archive)